USE AND ACTION

OF

STAYS AND CORSETS,

ON

DISEASE & DEVELOPEMENT

OF

THE FEMALE FIGURE.

BY

W. HEMPSON DENHAM, M.R.C.S.

LONDON:

JOHN CHURCHILL, PRINCES STREET, SOHO.

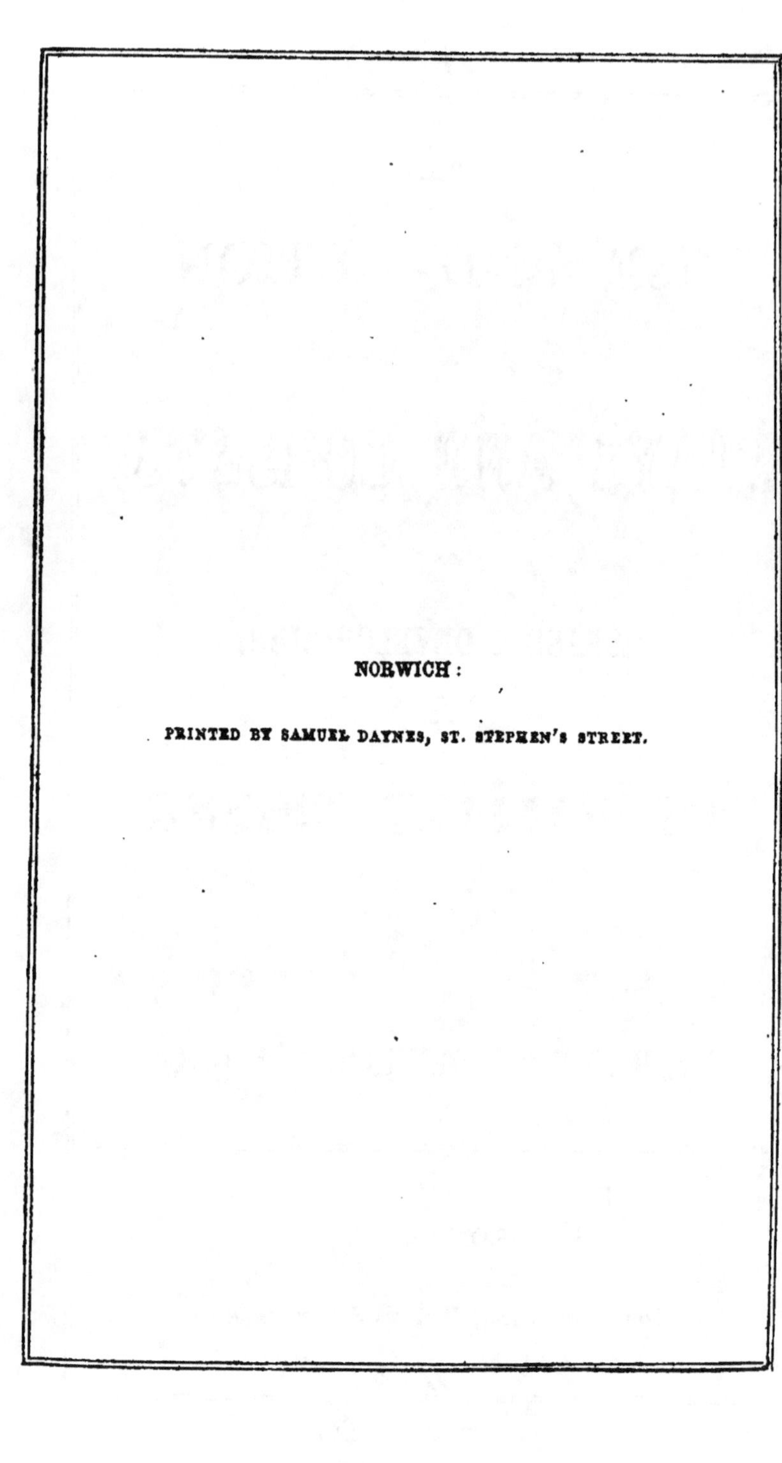

NORWICH:

PRINTED BY SAMUEL DAYNES, ST. STEPHEN'S STREET.

PREFACE:

IT *does not seem to me that a medical practitioner is stepping from the strict path of professional enquiry, when he investigates a subject of such general reference as that which forms the title of the present essay. Doubtless, however, there will always be some persons, in and out of the profession, who think, or profess to do so, that a medical practitioner should confine his criticisms and his labours, to merely diagnostic matters of disease, and not turn his attention to special enquiries on questions of individual, though of general concern. They would, too, if they could, curtail the exercise and influence of his pen, and not permit it to be used beyond the limits prescribed by their own contracted, self-sufficient, views.*

> *These unbelieving priests would urge the nation,*
> *To take their own specific for salvation.*

To revel in the airy regions of literature and fancy, to indite a tale, or to concoct a verse ; above all, to indulge in what they sapiently call " Utopian" ideas of change, are, in the minds of these people, such heterodox ideas for " a doctor" to indulge in, that they will scarcely give him, who resolutely rebels against their assumed conceptions of right, credit for possessing, like themselves, the ordinary attributes of physical existence.

iv.

To see these learn'd savans, with mouths that ope so wide,
To form a deep, dark cavern, in the which might hide
A coach, you'd guess Old Boguy, *as it seems he does,*
Concocts, and then destroys, their true " phonetic nuz.*"*

 According to the orthodoxy of some of these gentlemen, it is not only very undignified to prepare a pill and to compound a draught, but to do many other things that the necessities and usages of society require, and, requiring, sanction. For myself, I am not, at present, a convert to any such creed as theirs, being convinced that the whole tendency of human thought and action is against such doctrine. Nor do I look upon it as derogatory to professional " dignity," to investigate whatever is of general concern, or promotes the health and safety of the community.

 If the benevolence of a physician, or his presumed regard for the welfare of his patient, be to cease with consulting about a prescription and pocketing the fee, his enlarged beneficence, and his general usefulness, must be as empty as his title, and clearly proves that the days of " big wig-ism" have not yet passed. But there is, if I mistake not, a growing impression in the public mind, that usefulness is more valuable than frittering show; and if I read the state of things correctly, there is also a desire to receive suggestions of benefit from any one who can shew, with reason and justice, that previous impressions of either men or things have been wrongly entertained. It is admitted, however, to be more easy to find fault than to correct; to point out deficiencies than to suggest improvements. But although the denunciation of a particular subject, such an one for example as that under review, may not be thought by some to be genuine criticism of its real merits, still, the very act of canvassing its tendencies must be good in itself, for it will lead to its powers being refuted or confirmed by the efficient ordeal of general examination. To this tribunal will I willingly leave to decide the merits or demerits of the question I have openly canvassed, being convinced of the truthfulness, efficiency, and power of the tribunal appealed to. If, in the exercise of its jurisdiction, courtesy and conviction induce it to say as I say, be assured I shall respond bravissimo. *If it don't, why then I can but cast a glance of " dignified" astonishment at its sheer stupidity; and should I, on another occasion, have to seek its arbitrating power again like, a prudent lawyer I will take care, before entrusting my cause to its judgment, to find out what the final decision of the arbitrator will be.*

The reader may respond, Amen.

W. H. D.

THE USE AND ACTION, &c.

Fashion is every thing in the present world, and has some little influence in preparing us for the next. But, in nothing has the force of fashion ever been more strongly seen, than in the universal adoption of stays and corsets, as a necessary part of female attire.

If we take up a pair of stays and dissect them minutely, we must be thoroughly astonished that so queer an article of dress should be so generally used. What else upon earth but their very selves are they in any way shaped like? I know of nothing in this material world of ours, of so odd a cut. In their very form, like Punch's hump, they have not a compeer.

Nescio sit qualis in cælo terraque.

But then their use—this is always negative; often really and positively bad. If, as an anatomist, I were about to describe the human figure, or one of its detachments, I need not be at a loss wherewithal to compare the organization before me. In that complicated, yet simple, and beautiful structure, we have all nature's primitive and choicest forms—mechanical, optical, and physical. But a pair of stays! What on earth are they like?

Impar comparande mihi post nullos sodales,

Broad, narrow, and broad again! A double, an inverted cone! Whoever saw such a thing? Where in this world, or in any other, is the like form to be found? Etna inverted on the top of Mount Blanc—the Little Skyrryd on the larger Sugar Loaf! What a state of things! Has any one seen it? Then their separated parts—culled from the productions of most opposite climes—the air, the earth and the sea—cut and trimmed and stitched to form a bothering, aggregated, whole. How strange! Yet women like them; like them of course, because they wear them. Proof positive this, for whoever heard of women persisting in what they do not like! They like them, then—to say otherwise is useless. They are the veriest pet article of female attire; of woman in every state, high, low, and between; gay, retiring, domestic, and blue stocking.

But a girl without stays. Absurd, quite! She could not live an instant; and if she did, which, to be sure, is possible, she would not be half so interesting to herself, or to any one about her, for she would lose all tendency to those sweetly exciting hysterical fits that mama looks at, papa stares at, and which so surprise, frighten and astonish lovers—oh the sawneys, they're not yet in the secret—that they are ready to run in breathless haste and anxiety for half a score doctors to come quickly, in less than no time, as Paddy would have it, for the really loved one is certainly dying. Poor girl, she'll be a long while about it, that is, if she's a sensible girl, as all girls should be, and as some girls are.

Well. A doctor, the doctor, a dozen doctors go--the rest are out, hunting, fishing, shooting, gossiping, or driving on real journeys to imaginary patients, like—" *to bleed the mile-stone!* " They are out any rate. What should keep them at home? They wont read; they don't write, and what are they to do? And who would be cruel enough to kill doctors of ennui? They are out at any rate, but one of them it is presumed sees the patient soon. A moment's glance shews him the real state of things. He need not put any questions, if he have a head upon his shoulders, though he will do it perhaps for form's sake. A youngster, however, might mistake the thing; the man of experience, never. Coolly and quietly he scans his patient; views the physiognomy; the general contour. These tell the tale. With provoking quietude of manner—apparent indifference, not real—he sends the patient to bed, for she probably has been screaming hitherto on a couch or chair. She goes; and the act implies removal of the cause, though the effect continues; continues from induced habit in the part affected, and till remedies have had time to shew their potency.

The state of things thus induced can be easily traced, in very many instances, to the habit of wearing stays. The disordered condition above described, not unfrequently comes on after a hearty meal, and, *ergo*, presto, is the conclusion jumped at, that the meal, or a part of it, a something, an unknown, invisible, sort of guessed at something, though the stomach liked it at the time—be it peas, cabbage, salad, pastry, or meat—has disagreed and produced the state depicted. Wonderful peas! Extraordinary cabbage!! Marvellous salad!!! Astonishing pastry!!!! More singular meat!!!!! Yet able to produce such a remarkable state of things, with only one person amongst, perhaps, a family of ten. But this accusation of ingesta, is, in reality, fudge—all fudge. I don't believe a word of it, and I hope gentle reader you will doubt about it too.

Is such a creed consistent with common sense—a sufficient explanation of the real *causa rerum?* Nature made all these things, and having made them, intended them for people to eat—why then should people not eat them? There is no reason why they should not, *if they will but observe the laws that nature made when she made those things.* But if, with determined opposition to her well-concocted laws, a person choose to partake of the articles named, and then by tightly girding the ribs, or otherwise confining them, to tie up both ends of the stomach, that escape of its contents is impossible, who is to be surprised that constriction of one part should cause determination of blood to another, and produce disorder, and perhaps disease. *Cæteris paribus* to what more likely organs would such determination of blood in probability tend, in a young and excitable female, than to the uterine system? The developement of that system, and the restrained employment of its functions, alike increase the tendency, and the result is seen   Hence, then, the symptoms, caused as above stated.   But the whole gravamen of the charge is put down by patient, doctor, and by attendants, to the secret operation, ormalignity of some supposed undigested, and indigestible article, though no proof of its passing the *prima viæ*, in a state of crudity, is even afterwards to be had. A tolerably conclusive proof of the absurdity of the charge, and that it is uttered only as a cloak to ignorance.   It si strange, however, that those who are capable of thinking should not do so for themselves, and, instead of pinning their faith inconsiderately to the dicta of other men, should not desire commonsense to lead them, and strike out a path of thought and action for their personal guidance.

After a meal, a certain quantity of gas is generated by the most healthy stomachs. This is a perfectly natural process, and results no doubt, in part at least, from the food being resolved into its ultimate elements.   But, in the case alluded to, this but adds to the evil ; makes the compression of stays more intensely felt, and the consequent engorgement of viscera the sooner appreciable.

In a healthy condition of system, the gas thus generated, passes off with ease and safety, and produces nothing but that proper state of mechanical distension of the bowels for which it was designed, and which is necessary I believe to the proper performance of chymification. But not so when disease or other interference with nature's process, 'changes the condition from the healthy state.. Then it is that pain and other undesirable symptoms are produced, and the patient suffers, though she knows not why.   The cause, too, perhaps is allowed to go on, and then people become-astonished, that disease engendered, and made persistent, by their ignorance or imprudence, is not speedily got rid of, by the combined influence of physic, and change.   This is an exceedingly usual cockneyfied idea, and prevails to an almost absurd extent,with a certain class of Londoners.   One has often seen first and second class men from a city Ἐμπόριον, rusticating for a month or two, continually or at intervals, at some favourite spot between Gravesend and Brighton, committing all sorts of absurdities for their souls' and bodies' health, sitting up night after night, beyond a reasonable hour, stuffing, cramming, smoking, swearing, drinking, and then express themselves as utterly bewildered and unable to explain how the much coveted " change of air" has not done them any good. Wonderful, indeed !‖ But so, too, often is it, in another way, with unthinking girls. They wear stays utterly unfit to be located on their tender frames, and are then surprised, because they take physic occasionally, that their health is not good, nor their strength like Sampson's.

It is curious to trace the history of stays, and the wonderful transformations it has gone through, from its primitive form and intention to its present state. Originally nothing more than a belt, for the mere purpose of supporting the abdomen on certain trying and important occasions, it has been cut and twisted into every conceivable variety of form, and become, by use, an almost indispensable part of female attire. The concoctor of the article would look with astonishment on the cuts and twists modern science has given it, and would wonder how there could possibly be such a difference of taste, and style, and shape, between the women of his day, and our modern angels. At that time, it was little better than treason for men to see these things, and it was only the resolutely enquiring few who were permitted to explore the secret arcana of woman's then mystical being, to record the history of this wonderful habiliment.

The times, however, are changed now ; and the enthusiastic explorer of the good, the beautiful, and the useful can either spend his hour in critical examination at the windows of numerous artistes, or by doing the polite to some pretty little marchande behind the counter, may prove the extent of his taste as an ardent connoisseur, and become initiated into all the mystery of the curious employment, its history, and progress.

In the early days of stay-making, that is, when the
" noble science " was quite in its infancy, the having in-
fants was about the only reason for having stays. Woman
then, was unsophisticated in her thoughts and ways. She
had a strong constitution, and a hardy frame, and wanted
not nick-knackery to make it hardier. She relied upon
herself. Would she had ever done so ! She will do so
again, and be happier yet.

That was truly the iron age of womanly progression,
and as she passed *gradatim, seriatim, et literatim*, from
her then primitive state to the present golden era, her
wants unfortunately,imperceptibly increased,and with other
wants she wanted—a change of stays. Well, she had her
want supplied, but even then she was not easy—women
sometimes are not—for she observed, or, at any rate, it was
observed by those whose duty and happiness it was to do
so for her, that the very want she had just supplied,
brought with it the reality of another. This was a far
more serious one, for it referred to health, a thing not
lightly to be treated of, and though always coveted, is sel-
dom really or permanently possessed, and never sufficiently
valued. The real cause of the disordered state was overlooked, but the effect dragged its slow length along till it
gradually made woman what she was not intended to be,
an unnaturally susceptible and enervated subject.

This original and unique shape of woman's favourite,
pet, garment was no longer suited to her altered condition,
and in time was changed. One of the earliest changes
that the garment underwent, was the being made nearly
double the width it had previously been. This was soon
found to be more an inconvenience than otherwise, and
was altered too. At that time it was not usual to have
the ordinary " busk " in front; and so far, as there was
much less probability of injury resulting from the use of
stays, the absence of the busk was a positive benefit. But
the disagreeable occurrence of stays rucking up soon suggested the idea of additional comfort, from proper exten-
sion of the article in wear, and a " busk " was added, but

of a size and thickness at first, that would thoroughly astonish all modern wearers. Up to this period, the lace does not seem to have been added, but the fastening was made by tapes or strings.

The first " busk " would seem to have been a curious invention. It was of wood, and in size and thickness not very unlike the back of a modern chair; but at that time " wood," the Green Woods of Old England, were scattered abundantly over our loved, and cherished, and happy soil. There were none of your modern notions and necessities then, of weeding out the hedge rows, that the glaring sun may half cook the weary traveller on his tiresome journey. Wood and shade in those palmy days of mirth, innocence and jollity were abundant; the former, sufficiently so to come even to the aid of the useful stay maker. But in these ideal days of rail-road whirling, and politic expediency, horses are scarce—made scarcer by taxation—and there is no possibility now, as in days of yore, of stopping on a lengthened journey, to rest and revel in the grassy shade. In these degenerate days, one can only imagine with what ardent enthusiasm Virgil wrote and sung his soul-stirring, beautiful strain, on pastoral simplicity and enjoyment.

> *Tityre, tu, patulæ recubans sub tegmine fagi,*
> *Silvestrem tenui musam meditaris avena :*
> *Nos patriæ fines, et dulcia linquimus arva ;*
> *Nos patriam fugimus : tu, Tityre, lentus in umbra,*
> *Formosam resonare doces Amaryllyda sylvas.*

At that time, despite the actions of Roman plunderers, and since, a travelling cit could snatch a momentary enjoyment of pleasurable rest and retirement, within the shady precincts of a wide-spreading beech tree. But, alas, those days are gone, gone at the unbending dictum of a grasping commercial acquisitiveness, and we have not now even wood enough to spare for the ordinary necessities of woman—hollow expediency compelling her to the use of iron. Yes, modern " busks " are of steel. Fancy with what instinctive horror, in days gone by, woman would have shrunk from such a display of her iron rule. But what horrid expedients, alas, do not necessity ahd " science " familiarize the use of.

" *To what strange uses may we not come, Horatio.*"

It was not long before the lace was invented. This was, doubtless, a great step in the onward progress.

We next find stays, instead of being made in one entire piece, as hitherto, sloped, shaped, gusseted, and grooved, a piece or two at a time, till they gradually approached to modern notions of perfectibility of stay making But it was not till comparatively recent times, that it was found desirable to insert so many portions of bone, to support the figure, that a woman now must feel herself incased in the unyielding skeleton of a tiny whale. It is impossible that the effect of this can be otherwise than prejudicial, especially upon young, uninvigorated, frames.

Although I will not go so far as to say that I altogether disapprove of anything being worn by females, which from its tendency to promote personal comfort it may be thought desirable to give the name of stays,

" *A rose by any other name will smell as sweet.*"

Still I must record my opposition to the present construc tion that passes uuder that name, because distortion and disease can be clearly traced to the habit of wearing it; so much so, that it is a matter of astonishment, that mo- thers especially, with their proverbial affection for their offspring, should not long since have brought themselves to think much more upon the subject, and to enquire if stays be absolutely necessary to health and appearance.

A nicely proportioned and expanded female figure is very beautiful to behold; but this beautiful appearance can easily be obtained without the intervention of stays, at all. On the contrary, a lifeless, ugly, wooden doll—an inanimate figure—an insensate stick, can be so dressed up by the help of pads, and stays, and buckram, that it will assume a tolerably respectable looking form. But that a human female, a breathing, life-giving being, should be disguised by using continually and voluntarily these useless, ill-made, and often worse fitting garments is so remarkably strange, that it could not be believed, if it were not seen and known.

History some day or other will record the circumstance that stays were in general use, with all classes of society, as late as the middle of the nineteenth century ; that they gradually got out of favor and fashion, despite the strong prejudice enlisted in their favor amongst the unthinking; and that their use was altogether obsolete soon after that period, except with fishermen's wives in the Orkneys and Hebrides, the women of Kamschatka who had just adopted them, and with those in distant parts of Russian Siberia.

Certainly a good figure cannot possibly require the aid of stays, and it is equally certain that a really bad one cannot be improved by their constant use. As well might a scientific surgeon think of merely putting " irons " on the distorted legs of a ricketty child, as to think of improving the disfigured form of an adolescent girl, by continuing for that purpose the use of stays. In the first case, if he were really what his name implies, he would know well enough, that the external support could not add the elements of health and solidity to the bending bones of his distorted patient, but that those elements must come from the better resources and suggestions of his more perfect art. He would see the means that would be required—that science would point out for the peculiar condition he had to treat, and seeing them, it would be his duty, as it would be his desire, to combine those means with the employment of merely mechanical aid, if the latter seemed absolutely necessary to the efficiency of the former. That, however, would be but a mere contingency; a contingency that probably would not be acted upon at all.

As it would be with the treatment of the case just alluded to, so too, would it be with that of a young female,
who had disease or disorder from other,constutional, causes,
than the wearing stays.   The scientific surgeon would not
resort to agents that would, in all probability make matters worse, by moulding the still yielding bones into unnatural forms; but knowing of better means, would cast
aside the interference of stays altogether, and treat the
case, as he could safely and with more certainty do, by
the efficient means of his useful calling.   It is in these
cases more particularly, that the discrimination of the
surgeon is put to the test ; because he has to decide between disease occurring from other causes, and that which
I assert will be found on examination to be produced, in
some instances solely, and in others mainly, from wearing
stays.   If in the one case, he prescribed additional
" support" from the routine machine maker, his patient
must inevitably go on to still greater distortion and to
her grave.   While on the other hand, the treatment he
would judiciously employ, if had recourse to in time,would
shew, by partial or entire return of health, the magic in;
fluence and efficiency of art.

To those who have been accustomed to wear stays for a
considerable period, and whose prejudices have long been
enlisted in their favor, it would probably be very disagreeable at first, to leave them off; for, apart form the support
they are supposed to give, but which a healthy frame has
no right to require, the warmth they concentrate and im-
part to the surface must be exceedingly missed when it is
taken away.   But if women will but bring themselves to
see that this is the only evil, and that an imaginary one,
that can possibly result from throwing stays aside altoge-
gether, there can be little doubt of the course they will
pursue, and of the ultimate benefit that will arise from
adopting it.

Those medical practitioners, whose lot it has been to
be much consulted in diseases of the chest, must often
have seen the " round backed " girl, with protruding

shoulders, and possibly slight spinal deviation, gradually led on, from bad to worse, till she have become the victim of incurable phthisis, or equally incurable spinal disease. These effects, in many instances, can be traced to the direct action of stays, producing the very condition they were designed to prevent, namely, distortion of the muscles and bones of the chest and back. It has often happened to me to trace these effects upon the tolerably healthy; but still more frequently have I seen the delicate and " scrofulous " become the victims of fashion and habit.

The ill effects that stays thus produce, can be easily understood by looking at the anatomical construction of the chest, and the important organs it was formed to protect.

The chest may be considered as an expanding, cone-like, cavity, with its base below, the apex above, covered and protected by variously acting muscles, and by the arms. The latter, if not absolutely necessary to the perfect expansion of the chest, materially aid the performance of that important function, It is highly necessary, then, that the proper action of these should not be interfered with permanently by stays and bandages.

The apex of the chest, for our present purpose, may be considered as a fixed point; the base and sides as the expanding portions. Conveniently situated, on different parts of the chest, are larg eand effective muscles to produce the expansion. For those muscles to act sufficiently and naturally, they should be unrestrained by tight bandages and clothing. The effect of such things must be irregular, and perverted, action of the moving power, the] muscles. Muscles, from what ever cause, when forced to pull in a direction different to their ordinary course, must of necessity draw the bones and ligaments of the joints into strained and unnatural states. These unnatural attitudes, if frequently repeated, in a system in any way prone to disease, are but too apt to bring into undesired activity, that tendency to unhealthy action, which would otherwise have been latent, and which in many instances, with care, would never become developed at all. What, too, can be more reasonable than that a forced and strained action of the ligaments connecting the ribs to the back bone, should first of all excite that subacute degree of inflammation which characterizes disease in structures of their low vitality, and subsequently absorption or distortion of bones, with the other usually long train of ills. The wonder is, that these things do not more frequently happen than they do. Their not occurring, in every instance in which the means are used to excite them, merely proves the strong counteracting power of nature, and her abhorrence of disease, and how much she tries to keep our vain humanity free from the evils of self-imposed disorder.

The chest contains and guards the heart and lungs, the most important organs of the animal frame. Nature in her beautiful and perfect schemes for the happiness of the human race, and the integrity of health, foreseeing the all-important part that the heart and lungs must perform in man's organization, placed them in a situation of far greater security than she considered some other parts would be likely to require.

The very fact that nature has taken such especial pains to guard these parts from harm, ought undoubtedly to make us cautious in the extreme how we, for mere fashion's sake, endanger the performance of the healthy function of organs that nature has been so careful to protect. Yet, despite nature's indications for caution, fashion and habit have so worked their way into the actions of man's better half, that she often, for vain appearance sake, thwarts nature's kindliest efforts to keep herself and her offspring in healthy form. But this is " fashion."

Surely fashion must have had its origin in the wonderfully wicked designs of a certain well-known " gentleman in black," who, from sheer spite, perhaps, because man admires the beautiful form of Eve's lovely daughters, must have instilled into their minds some evil desire to punish man's presumption, by urging them to a habit of self distortion, upon some such principle as that which induced a lady, whose husband loved her for her beautiful ankles, to go into one of the London Hospitals and, feigning disease, to have one of her legs amputated, because, having quarrelled with her husband, she was fully determined he should no longer be gratified by admiring their form! Wonderful infatuation? The more wonderful because it is true.

If stays were always made in accordance with the physiological developements of the human figure, it is very possible they would not do harm; but then they would be utterly useless for every purpose of support, as well as for that one for which they seem specially desired, the giving a "genteel" appearance to the general form. But this "gentility" of person after all, with even the extraneous addenda of stays and pads is a very relative quality, a kind of imaginary nonentity, without a standard to judge from. Yet certain it is, that she in whom nature has implanted that pleasing condition, whatever her position in the social state may be, is never likely to be able either to lose or to disguise it, though arrayed in nothing but sackcloth and ashes. But when we see stays, as in almost every instance we do, made solely for the purpose of affording compression, it is morally certain that their chief effect must be a bad one. Many a time have I seen the not, perhaps, thoroughly healthy girl of seventeen or eighteen, just budding into beautiful womanhood, wearing stays as utterly unfit for her expanding form to be dressed in, as it is possible to conceive. Indeed it is not an uncommon circumstance to see such a girl dressed out in stays which, to say the least, can only be worn with safety by one who is several years her junior. This is precisely the circumstance from which the greatest injury results. This is the time of life and constitutional condition when the worst effects may be expected, if the state described be allowed to go on unheeded and unchecked.

Such a state of things cannot do otherwise than produce distortion. Nature, with kindliest effort, may struggle resolutely against the attempt; but nature, driven from her course of true benevolence, must always yield, when animal and vital power are opposed to the continued action of mechanical force.

The disobedience offered to the legitimate action of nature's physical laws, induces her to resent the insult given to her decree. She does this, like a well judging omniscient being, prescient of what is right, and confident of her own unfailing powers and judgment when not improperly opposed; but pained to see her laws unheeded and infringed by vanity and ignorance. She *does*, however, resent the insult offered by disobedience to her benignant rule, and she does it, not by storms from heaven to frighten the foolish, or by working miracles to astonish the thoughtless, but by withdrawing from the struggle her protective, but unappreciated, power, the *vis medicatrix naturæ*, and allowing full force and action to the silly efforts of those who think they know better than herself. Distortion of person, and disease of structure, are the mode of punishment she adopts to bring vanity and ignorance to an acknowledgment of their error; and though she cannot, perhaps, be said with truth, literally to inflict the conditions described, yet they come by her permissive power, gradually, thoroughly, and as certainly, as destruction follows the earthquake.

In the construction of stays, a central wooden or metallic busk is believed to be a necessary element. The direct pressure exerted by this substance, is from the centre of the breast bone, to from five to seven inches along the abdomen. This, as a means of pressure or support, would of course be useless without the counteracting power of the lace behind. Now it almost invariably happens when a new pair of stays is placed on the figure that the edges will not meet behind by several inches, and often it is only by inserting the fingers resolutely between each interstice of the lace, giving " a good pull, a strong pull, and a pull altogether," that the edges of the stays can be made to approximate. I have many times been forced to witness on different subjects the reality of this, when it has been necessary to denude the patient for accurate examination. Then it is that the unpleasant truth is forced upon the mind that want of judgment, and obstinate adherence to fashion, make sad havoc occasionally with sometimes the naturally best of forms. It is as common as possible on such occasions to behold the skin creased and indented by the pressure of the tightly-laced and misfitting stays, the surest possible indication of what has been going on, and what may be expected. Indeed external appearances are often sufficient to point out with certainty what will be disclosed by more minute examination.

A case in point to illustrate my meaning, may not be misplaced; but as I do not wish to occupy space by detailing needlessly cases that must assimilate [very closely to each other, the following as a specimen of the condition met with, shall suffice for the present. I was lately consulted by Miss ———— between 16 and 17 years of age, in consequence of the shoulders " growing out." On undressing the patient to examine her condition, the following appearances presented themselves :—the anterior edges of both scapulæ, were more inward than natural, whilst the bases were outward and more posteriorly. On dropping a " plumb line " from the upper part of the curix to the pelvis behind the dorsal vertebræ, were seen to have deviated three-fourths of an inch from their proper course. The skin on the back and sides presented almost innumerable red creases or furrows, indicating the action of a compressing agent. On examining this young lady's stays, sufficient was soon visible to mark the cause of the change. The shoulder straps, when the stays were laced, instead of being so placed as to allow of the proper adduction of the shoulders and arms in front, acted like the surgical figure - of - eight bandage, for fractured clavicles, and drew the shoulders backward. The scapulæ were necessarily everted as described, and formed the " growing out," related above. There was a little inaccuracy in the performance of the digestive functions about the patient, sympathetic with the state induced. This was corrected by such means as readily suggested themselves, and under the influence of these, cold sponging, and the shower bath, preparatory to sea bathing, the young lady, having as I directed thrown her stays aside, has recovered health, and in due time, by perseverance, will lose her deformity too.

The condition of this young lady would have varied but little, had she been accustomed to wear stays of the last new fashion, made without shoulder straps. This recent innovation on the established shape, is scarcely worthy to be called an improvement. It is, however, a tacit admission of the justice of my sarcasm; but while it looks like an unwillingness to relinquish the use of the article entirely, it shews an evident dissatisfaction with the present form, and indicates conviction of a baneful result.

One of the surest evidences that stays misfit the figure, is to be found in the condition that is often pointed to with some little exultation as a proof of quite the contrary state. This is in the ability to pass the hand, on the hand of another person, between the laced stays and the back bone. That this can be done with a well-fitting article, is not meant to be denied, but it is as certainly effected by one of an opposite description, the difference being that it is permanent in the one case, and transitory in the other. In the former, it is a condition brought on by a voluntary effort for a particular purpose, and it is not there fore to be taken as a correct indication of the actual state. In the latter, the condition is a permanent one, so long as the stays are worn, brought about and continued solely by compression. When the individual wishes to produce that state, which is often done from a desire to shew that the stays are suitable to her condition, she voluntarily brings into action the large trapezoid, and other muscles in their locality, that act specially or principally on the shoulders and shoulder blades; and with the assistance of other muscles that act upon the trunk, she throws the abdomen forward, the shoulders backward, and a deep furrow is consequently formed in the very centre of the back, along which it is quite possible to thrust an ordinary hand. But this condition, induced as it is by a voluntary effort, lasts no longer than the muscles, tired of the irksome strain, seek to relax themselves. They are enabled to do this, because when voluntary action ceases, there is nothing to prevent the return of their natural condition. But when, as in the latter case, compression is the cause of the state induced, the muscles are so far passive in the matter, that they only act as they are induced by the exciting agent, or sympathetically perhaps with other parts, but their disordered action and the state resulting from it, become gradually persistent.

When ill-adjusted stays have been worn some time, the the condition just alluded to, is the inevitable result. A little reflection and reference to the figure, will elucidate all this with tolerable correctness. The eighth, ninth, and tenth ribs are connected to the breast bone, by long pieces of semi-circular formed cartilage. The design of this curious formation was to provide for greater increase in the expanding power of the chest, and was a most beautiful constructive idea of the Deity. But this very form, beautifully adapted as it is to its intended use, is but ill suited to one for which it was never designed, and therefore cannot bear with impunity continued compression.

It happens that the part just alluded to is precisely the spot where the chief pressure of stays is made. The consequence of continued pressure in this part, must absolutely be to bring together the unopposed edges of the cartilages in front. This approximation of the cartilages must necessarily exert pressure on the contents of the thoracic and abdominical cavities. The liver, stomach, and bowels become pressed upon. These in their turn, press up the diaphragm, and this, again the heart and lungs. The ribs subjected to the tightly-laced garment, are compelled to yield in one direction or another, and the result is the contracted, pigeon shaped, chest depicted above. But if, on the contrary, it happen that the susceptibility of the back part of the chest be greater than the other, we then find inflammation set up in the articulating surfaces of the ribs and spine. Large and important nerves of motion, sensation, and involuntary action, being there in the immediate neighbourhood of the disease as it progresses, not unfrequently participate in the disordered condition, and I believe I have often traced satisfactorily, and clearly, some of the anomalous disorders of females, which we frequently meet with, to this fertile and efficient, but unrecognised, disturber of the health. Shortness of breath, with palpitation of the heart, and other disturbances of the circulation, are produced from the mechanical displacement of, or interference with, the viscera just named; and more than one instance has occurred within the author's knowledge, in which death has been produced, during the excitement of the dance, from no other apparent cause than this.

Fortunately the ill effects resulting from the use of improperly constructed stays, do not always proceed thus far; and then amongst the more usual and certain consequences to be observed, are disordered health, more or less permanent, but not always satisfactorily explained or understood, protrusion of the shoulders, weakness of the spine, tendency to Hernia from the abdominial strain, and engorgement of the viscera, abdominal, cranial, and thoracic.

It is not at all an unusual thing with some of our medical literati to attribute all this, but ill understood, condition to the influence of the scrofulous constitution of the individual. Yet singularly enough it has never struck their learned minds as rather inexplicable, that in a large family of children, disease will thus attack the girls and never touch the boys. This circumstance alone ought to have been sufficient to make medical practitioners look more thoroughly into the real cause of disease, and not content themselves with repeating the crude theories of other men, as dogmatic to be received and implicitly believed, without critical enquiry into their actual truth. The evils resulting from this ready and often ignorant assumption of the poisonous action of the scrofulous state, as the only means of explaining what in reality is misunderstood, are really very great. Whole families have been distressed and made miserable by it; have become marked objects for unjustly applied scorn; been looked upon as contaminated beings to be seen only to be shunned, for all purposes of social relation; sweepingly denounced as " eaten up " with scrofula, when a great deal at least of the so-called scrofulous state, can be clearly traced to the bad habits of dressing, but to nothing more positively than to the continued use of improper stays.

Ought any one to be surprised, when two such important organs as the heart and lungs become mechanically interfered with, that parts to which their influence more immediately extends, should sympathize with their state, and become, if possible, more than morbidly prone to inveterate disease? It would be wonderful if it were not so. It is equally marvellous that it is not frequently more so. But who can controul fashion and inveterate habit? The moral philosopher and the politician may attempt it; but the task is a difficult one and not easily accomplished. Fashion is all powerful, and women love to follow it. One thing, however, is certain it has not hitherto been fashionable with " fashionable physicians," to write down the follies and vanities of the world. They have striven rather to uphold them. True they have written books without number, and sometimes borrowed ideas, without acknowledgment, from every brain but their own, apparently to verify the true sarcasm of Byron,

> " 'Tis pleasant sure to see one's name in print,
> A book's a book, although there's nothing in't."

But the natural good sense of women, and the stimulus that now-a-days is given to the free exercise of thought, it is to be hoped will soon get rid of much of fashion, that so prejudicially affects themselves, and induce them to see, and seeing to act upon the impression, that the nearer approach the perfect developement of body and *mind*, hich nature designed them to have and enjoy, the more estimable they will become in the eyes of that portion of the other sex whose good opinion and affections are worth having, the *ne plus ultra* on earth of what women can desire.

> " *Beauties in vain their pretty eyes may roll,*
> *Charms strike the sight, but merit wins the soul.*"

The first aim and object of dress should be protection of the person, without offering restraint to muscular power, or to the exercise of the respiratory function. This object attained, the next design should be to keep the surface and extremities sufficiently warm in winter, and comfortably cool in summer. Anything superadded to these, as far as neatness of cut is concerned, that does not interfere with the primary object in view, cannot be objected to. The ingenuity of some of our *marchandes des modes* is really very great, and they have done their best to shew off with effect, pretty forms and faces, but they have not been equally regardful of nature and health. By far the greater part of the inventive powers of these ingenious persons has been exhausted in transforming the exterior articles of female attire, and it cannot be denied that much taste and judgment have been displayed of late in some of the changes that caprice or fashion has made. But it was not merely with regard to the exterior dress that change was required. It was equally wanted with more invisible garments; and it seems to me that considerable and very useful changes could easily be made in the construction of stays, and in the, at present, very ugly under petticoat, with reference especially to comfort and appearance. But as these suggestions might come more appropriately and effectively from those whose special province it is to " cut out " and manufacture articles for female wear, I shall refrain from enlarging on that particular topic, except merely to [add that whatever changes it may hereafter be thought desirable to make in articles of the sort, nature's intentions, with reference to the chest, must not be overlooked, or the *utile cum dulce* will not be combined.

Great credit is undoubtedly due to those whose province

it is to suggest changes of costume in the *beau monde* of fashion. Still it is clear that in many of those changes, the individuals alluded have been but copyists or modifiers of the inventions of their predecessors. Those who will take the trouble to review the costumes of the present and preceding reigns, and compare them accurately, will be convinced of this, and see how modern notions have squared and amalgamated with the ideas of the past, to reintroduce old friends with other names and faces. In this statement, no disparagement is meant to the ingenious devices of the persons concerned, but it is given as an illustration of the complexity of the subject, and how much more easy it is to alter than to invent.

The advocates for the use of stays would do well to make a comparative statistical analysis of the actual amount of deformity and disease that occurs in males and females. If this be done, the result is not very doubtful, nor that it will preponderate very unfavourably to the account of the latter. Where, and in what, is the cause of this opposite condition? The sound and the diseased in the persons under review, will be found to have both sprung from the same progenitorial stock. Can we then imagine *dissimilia similibus propagantur.*—The cause, if different, cannot, therefore in every instance, be progenitorial; but must be a subsequently acquired one. Where is its origin? In what does it consist? The orthodox doctrine of the day, I am aware, is, that the inactive bodily employments to which girls are subjected, produce the disorders from which they suffer. Yet inactivity of mind and body—of tongue and limb—is not natural to girls any more than to boys, and cannot be enforced on the healthy and the strong. Bodily inactivity, then, *vera vis inertiæ,* whenever it exists, should not be lightly regarded. It should be viewed not as a cause of disease, but itself as the result of some blighting influence being exerted on the system, by an occult agent not yet made manifest. Let the reader note the circumstance that he will invariably find when the circulation, the respiratory, and other animal functions have been improperly interfered with, by mechanical restraint on the expansion of the chest, that the state of inactivity, that absence of desire for motion and exertion alluded to above, will come on as the result. If, too, its cause be seen and known it will be looked upon, not as an evil, but as a positive good ; as a kindly monitor to remind the patient of her state ; as a proof of nature's watchful agency over our ways ; and of her extreme solicitude to avert the approaching evil by giving an early indication of a tendency to disease. It is very important that this early manifested condition, should not be overlooked or misunderstood, for it is the seed time of disorder ; but the experience of every practitioner who has seen much of disease in its chronic state, must convince him that many instances occur in which the condition mentioned, has not been estimated so rightly as it ought. This being the case, who can wonder that the treatment is not so successful as is always desired? Or that, when disease has progressed to organic change, become more and more obscured by the period of its continuance, and being bandied about perhaps from one to another, in a circle of half a dozen " fashionable doctors,'' the treatment in then its confirmed condition, should not succeed any better than before.

At no very distant period of time, stays, I believe will be so modified in form, and in the intention with which they will be used, that as far as the present garment is concerned, the use of it will be altogether obsolete. When woman has arrived at a certain stage of life, and is in the performance of functions for which she was designed, more especially during the time of lactation, it is much to her convenience to have a certain amount of support for the distended and secreting mammary glands. Again, after repeated instances of child bearing, it occasionally happens that the walls of the abdomen, from the previous disten sion they have undergone, remain so flaccid, that the viscera are consequently liable to displacement. A mechanical sustaining power is, therefore, necessary for such a condition. But the object sought under these peculiar circumstances, can never be obtained but very partially, if at all, by the aid of stays. Moreover, a far greater amount of assistance than stays are capable of affording, may be easily and efficiently had from other means.   This, however, is a question rather foreign than not to the one under review, and need not now be enlarged on.   My object is not so much to condemn the use of stays, with women whose bones have long been solidified, though even in such cases stays may be made to produce a great amount of mischief, as it is to censure their use at an earlier period of life.   The condemnation here given is suggested chiefly for the benefit of the growing girl, the adolescent woman, between the ages of fifteen and twenty five.   It is between these periods, but more especially under twenty years of age, that the injury complained of is so frequently seen.   At a later period of life, if injury have not yet shewn itself, it would be far more difficult to induce it then, than at an earlier period.   It must be almost extreme force to produce the effect at that particular time, and the result of this would soon shew itself in a way that would speedily compel the experimentalist to desist.   Besides women at that period of life have little reason to be particular about their shapes and waists.   In the majority of instances the object of life has long since been obtained, and women have then but little reason to speculate on the bare probabilities of the worldly future.

The undisputed fact that deformity of chest and spine frequently arises from constitutional causes, does not invalidate the force of the argument I have raised, that the disorder can often be clearly traced to the compressing action of stays.   A sand bank is not less a means of danger to the sailor in a storm, because a rock would sooner shatter his unmanageable barque.   Experience, in many instances very dearly bought, has taught him the reverse, and made him look with dread on both these agents as provocatives of ill.   So too with stays.   They are not written down as the sole producers of crooked spines and chests, but they are denounced as a means of frequently inducing disease in individuals who, but for their exciting agency, would never have suffered from certain of its forms.   Let the sceptic look amongst the individuals who compose the army, and see if he can meet in them with crooked spines and ribs. If, however, he will continue his search and look amongst the families of which these individuals are a part, he will be able to find many specimens of the disease occurring in the female branches, whilst the male division are altogether exempt. How is this explainable? The parents are the same, and by the physiological axiom, " that like begets like "—*similia similibus producentur*—the tendency to disease would be the same, with similar physical treatment, amongst sons and daughters. But did any one ever see a crook-backed soldier? He would be a strange looking subject at the Horse Guards, and the Park, and equally odd both at Osborne and Windsor. It cannot be said that the soldier is exempt from the varied ills of the so called scrofulous state. Judging from my own experience, I should say that scrofulous diseases, particularly opathalmia, are rather common amongst them, having myself seen several cases that had been discharged as incurable by the medical officers at Fort Pitt. These cases are said to be treated there by the ordinary routine of leeching, blistering, mercury, and cupping, but as might be expected, with little permanent benefit. An opposite mode of treatment generally puts them right.

The fact that soldiers are exempt from those diseases of the spine and chest that their sisters suffer from, makes the inference a fair one, that the cause of the exemption must be a different condition of physical training. It should be borne in mind, too, that this difference of training must have been in active operation before these men quitted the domestic circle to become adepts in drill. To what important difference of training, then, can this exemption from disease of the male branches, be ascribed, so reasonably and so justly, as to that of their not wearing articles of clothing to compress their ribs, and prevent respiration being free and efficient. If the difference of condition had not existed previously to the time of the men going to drill, a portion of the benefit might perhaps be ascribed to the manœuvres taught by the sergeant. But as the result existed long before the teaching of that omnipotent functionary, it is clear he cannot claim the benefit as his own, Further it may be laid down as an axiom, that if females will take care to have their chests unfettered, they will not require to be taught the antics that make the " awkward squad " so ludicrous at morning drill in the Park, in order to insure themselves healthy frames. It becomes, however, a painful circumstance to observe, when all the elements of worldly comfort are present, seemingly combined to make their possessor happy in her sphere, that disease unexpectedly steps in to mar her happiness. But it is doubly painful to be forced to believe that in many instances disease is heedlessly engendered by mere inattention to the simpliest precepts.

> " *First follow nature, and your judgment frame*
> *By her just standard, which is still the same :*
> *Unerring nature, still divinely bright,*
> *One clear, unchang'd, and universal light,*
> *Life, force, and beauty, must to all impart,*
> *At once the source, the end, and test of art.*
> *Art from that fund each just supply provides ;*
> *Works without show, and without pomp presides ;*
> *In some fair body, thus th' informing soul*
> *With spirits feeds, with vigour fills the whole,*
> *Each motion guides, and ev'ry nerve sustains*
> *Itself unseen, but in th' effects remains.*"

From the preceding remarks, perhaps the reader, like myself, will be induced to draw the following legitimate deductions :

That the use of stays is not necessary to health and comfort.

That they should never be worn by any female under the age of 24 or 25.

That deformity and disease frequently come on solely from wearing improper stays.

That where there is a tendency to protrusion of the shoulders in young girls, it will always be found that stays have been worn, and are the cause of the distortion.

That in the treatment of such cases, in addition to other means, it is of the utmost importance to abolish the use of stays altogether.

That public singers would obtain an immense acquisition of power and tone of voice, by abstaining continually from the use of stays.

That even at present many ladies have discarded the use of stays in summer, not only without being killed by the dreadful innovation on established custom, but with positive personal comfort to themselves.

That as some of the more sensible " better halves" of creation have thrown their stays aside, in summer time, *ergo*, other ladies may do the same ; and if in summer, then also in winter.

That by not wearing stays at all in the early period of life, the chest would become naturally and better developed—respiration would be stronger and more free— animal heat would be more certainly formed—there would be far less probability of disordered circulation, and congestion of the viscera—and, as a certain consequence, there would inevitably be a better state of health, a sound mind, and a well-formed body.

Such are the conclusions I have been forced to draw from examination of the subject. I believe them to be true. But if in every instance in which it has occurred to me to discuss the condition above described with a scientific friend, it has not invariably happened that I have made him a convert to all my views, this does not militate at all against the truthfulness of their character, but by analogical reasoning, might be negative proof to help to confirm them. For, one individual seeing disease apparent to his senses, and a constitution of body evidently disordered by the changes going on, might find sufficient perhaps to rivet his attention without travelling further back to unravel the deep mystery of real causation. To my view, however, of the subject, this is not all that science should seek to accomplish. Merely to correct or to cure an evil, be it bodily or social, I do not believe to be sufficient   Science should embrace a more extended range; and while she make use of every rational means to alleviate or to cure all mortal ills, she should direct her efforts, with equal zeal and care, to the intricate, important, but useful theme, the investigation of ultimate causes, and the *prevention* of disease.

THE END.

Norwich:

PRINTED BY S. DAYNES, ST. STEPHEN'S STREET.

May be had in Demy 8vo. price 3s. 6d. cloth,

VERBA CONSILII;

Or Hints to Parents who intend to bring up their Sons
to the Medical Profession.

BY

W. HEMPSON DENHAM, M. R. C. S.

———

On the motives which should guide a parent in
assigning a son to pursue the study of medicine,
Mr. Denham offers excellent remarks.—*Lancet.*

I have read your " Verba Consilii " with much
pleasure; half a dozen copies of it have already
passed through my hands.

Unsolicited letter to the author, from the late
J. G. Crosse, Esq., *Surgeon to the Norfolk and
Norwich Hospital.*

———

London : John Churchill, Princes' Street, Soho,
and all Booksellers.